My Dolly Dressing book of Fairies

Illustrated by Lisa Carr

How to dress your Fairies

❁ On the back cover you will find two dolls— Amber and Crystal.

❁ Ask an adult to use a pair of scissors to cut along the dotted lines.

❁ Carefully push out the dolls and their stands.

❁ Fit the stand into the slots at the bottom of the press-out doll so that she can stand up.

❁ On the inside pages, just press out the dolls' clothes and accessories.

❁ To dress the doll, simply fit the clothes tabs into the slots on the doll.

❁ Read **Fairies' Diary** to find out which clothes Amber and Crystal wear. The clothes will fit both dolls if they want to trade!

p

Fairies' Diary

In the springtime, there's plenty of **Spring Cleaning**. Everything needs to be dusted and repaired after the winter. Amber and Crystal change out of their fairy dresses to do their chores. Amber wears starry coveralls and Crystal wears poppy pants.

It's Midsummer Eve and all the fairies in the glade are getting ready for the **Midsummer Ball**. Amber and Crystal dress up in their favorite flowers. Amber wears a cornflower gown and Crystal wears a rose gown.

Harvest Time is an important time for the fairies. They work hard all year looking after the plants and flowers. In the fall, the results are the plump, juicy fruit and nuts in the woods. The weather is cooler, so Amber and Crystal wear warmer clothes in orange and red and yellow.

Harvest Time

maple leaf headdress

beechnut cap

red watering can

green watering can

maple leaf dress

beechnut dress

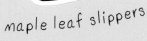
maple leaf slippers

beechnut slippers

Midsummer Ball

flower hair accessories

rosebud hat

cornflower wand

blue cornflower dress

rosebud ball gown

rosebud wand

white slippers with flowers

rosebud shoes

Spring cleaning

headscarf

broom

feather duster

poppy top

blue overalls with bright yellow stars and T-shirt

lilac fairy dress

poppy pants

fresh green fairy dress

blue and yellow sneakers

yellow and red sneakers

Halloween

pumpkin-shaped hat

witch's hat

jack-o'-lantern

witch's broomstick

pumpkin dress

witch's dress

pumpkin slippers

witch's boots

The Winter Ball

frosted tiara

sparkling wand with a purple handle

ice tiara

frosted blue ball gown with sparkling detail

sparkling wand with a frosted blue handle

purple ball gown with icy white detail

white frosted slippers

purple slippers

Sleep Tight

pale green
nightcap

candle

lantern

bluebell-colored nightcap

pale green
and white
nightgown
with
snowdrop
detail

white
nightgown
with
bluebell
detail

snowdrop-colored slippers

bluebell-colored slippers

Fairies' Diary

The fairies think it's lots of fun to dress up on **Halloween**. Crystal's decided to dress up in a pumpkin outfit. Amber's going to dress up as a witch!

The fairies will go to sleep for the winter. But before they do, they hold a splendid **Winter Ball**. The glade is decorated with special lights, and the bug orchestra plays dance music all night. Amber and Crystal spend weeks preparing their costumes for the Winter Ball. Amber and Crystal's gowns sparkle like frost.

The fairies get ready for their long winter sleep. Amber changes into her white-and-green snowdrop petal nightgown. Crystal pulls on her cozy bluebell nightgown. They won't wake up until the snow thaws. **Sleep Tight**!

Have fun, Bye!

Crystal xx   Amber x

Design your own
Fairy clothes

Use the patterns below to make your own fairy costumes. Trace from the pattern onto a piece of cardboard, color it, cut it out, and try it on. Then sit back and admire your fabulous creation!

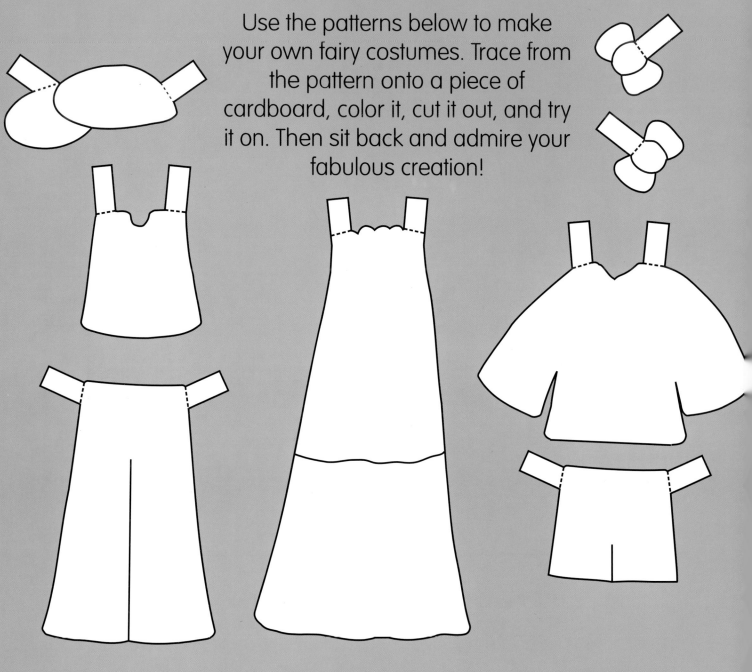

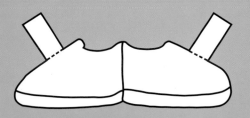